Stepping Through History

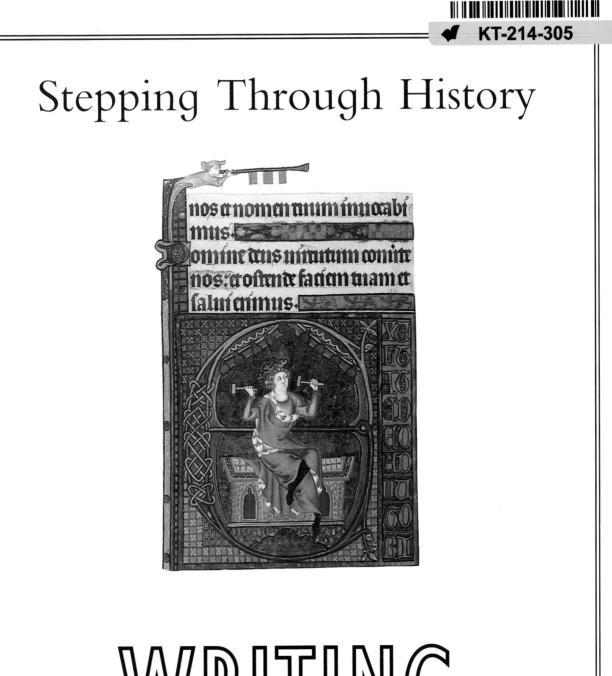

nos cr nomen tuum inuocabi
mus.
omine deus uimutum conite
nos: et oftende faciem tuam et
falui crimus.

WRITING

PEGGY BURNS

Wayland

Stepping Through History

Money
News
The Post
Shops and Markets
Travel
Writing

Editor: Vanessa Cummins
Series designer: John Christopher

© Copyright 1994 Wayland (Publishers) Limited

First published in 1994 by Wayland (Publishers) Limited
61 Western Road, Hove, East Sussex BN3 1JD, England

British Library Cataloguing in Publication Data
Burns, Peggy
Writing. – (Stepping Through History Series)
I. Title II. Series
411.09

ISBN 0-7502-1137-7

Picture Acknowledgments
The Publishers would like to thank the following for allowing their pictures to be used in this book:
Ann Ronan 15, 16 (above), 17, 22 (below), 27, 28 (above); British Telecom Museum 13 (Imperial War Museum);
Eye Ubiquitous 5; Image Select 23 (below); Mary Evans *contents,* 12, 19, 28 (below); Michael Holford *cover* (top), 4,
5 (above), 6, 7, 8 (below), 9, 14; Robert Harding 11; Parker Pens Ltd 20, 21 (below), 22 (above); Ronald Sheridan
10, 18, 24 (below), 26 (below); The Science Museum 24 (above); Tony Stone 11, 29; Wayland Picture Library *cover*
(right and left), *title,* 16 (left), 19 (below), 23 (above), *timeline* (top: Biblioteca Laurenzia), *timeline* (middle: British
Museum), *timeline* (bottom), Werner Forman 8 (above), 25, 26 (above).

Typeset by Strong Silent Type
Printed and bound in Italy by G. Canale & C.S.p.A, Turin

CONTENTS

Words found in **bold italic** in the main text are explained in the glossary.

WORDS IN PICTURES

Writing is a way of talking without speaking. When you read a book, you are reading the thoughts of the person who wrote it. It is as if that person – even if he or she is dead now – is speaking to you.

Writing originally developed from speech. People 25,000 years ago used grunts and gestures to pass messages to each other or express their feelings of fear or happiness.

Later, vocal sounds would be used to name objects and these sounds could be understood by other people. When sounds and names were linked marked the beginnings of spoken language.

Drawing developed when the first **Stone Age** people picked up pieces of bone or stone and made scratches on rocks. These early humans known as **Neanderthals** drew and painted beautiful pictures of animals and people on the walls of the caves where they lived. Ancient cave paintings have been found all over the world including, France, Spain, Australia, Russia and India. Drawing was just one step away from writing.

Later, cave painting used geometric shapes to show people and animals. These shapes were designed to pass on information to people. A simple message might read:

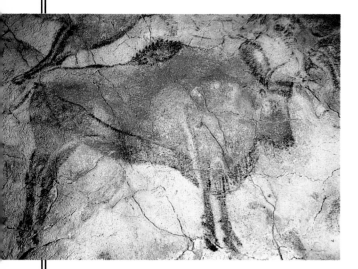

This cave drawing of a bison was found in northern Spain. It was drawn by cave dwellers over 14,000 years ago.

Pictograms could be used to keep records. This ancient tablet from Mesopotamia (now in modern-day Turkey) is a farming record, showing where crops were grown.

This would tell the person reading it, 'I am going to the woods to hunt. Back tonight.' Picture writing, or pictograms, were the very first form of writing.

The human memory is limited, so it is easier to remember things if they are written down. Years ago farmers needed to keep records of crops and animals, so they drew rough pictures of sheep, oxen and ears of barley. People needed to count off the days, weeks and years, so they invented signs that stood for numbers. As more uses for pictograms were discovered, more people learned to read and write.

Picture messages are so useful that many simple picture messages are still used today. For instance, a stick figure shown on a door represents a public toilet. Road signs are also pictograms and are often the same throughout the world. A wavy line means bends in the road ahead. Can you think of any more?

This Australian road sign is a modern pictogram. It warns that Kangaroos may be crossing the road.

THE FIRST WRITTEN LANGUAGE

This tablet from Sumeria was engraved with pictograms around 5,000 years ago. The first proper written language called 'cuneiform' developed from pictograms.

The Sumerians, an ancient people who lived in Mesopotamia (between the valleys of the Tigris and Euphrates rivers in the Middle East), were the first people to invent a written language. Around 5,000 years ago, they began to draw pictograms with reed styli (square-ended writing tools), on wet clay. The clay tablets were then hardened in the hot sun to preserve the drawings. The Sumerians sometimes drew pictograms on bone or metal instead of on clay.

Over a period of many years the pictograms changed as people began to use scribbled signs instead of the original, careful drawings. By 3,000 BC the Sumerians were using wedge-shaped writing called cuneiform ('cuneus' means 'wedge' in Latin). Cuneiform was quicker and easier to write than pictograms.

At first, there was a vast number of signs, over 2,000 in all. As time went on the number of signs was reduced to around 800, of which 200–300 were commonly used. The signs could also be used to write different languages.

This Sumerian statue was carved with cuneiform writing in 860 BC.

IDEAS, SOUNDS AND ALPHABETS

The ancient Egyptians lived in the Nile valley between 5,000 and 6,000 thousand years ago. Around 3000 BC they invented hieroglyphs – signs which stood for letters, words and ideas. Like cuneiform these signs also developed from pictograms.

Many of the signs were pictures of animals, birds and people and are recognizable today. Others stood for single sounds, but most Egyptian hieroglyphs stood for ideas. A picture of an eye with a tear coming from it was not the word 'eye'; it meant 'sorrow'. Idea symbols are known as ideograms.

Hieroglyphs were carved on limestone tablets. These hieroglyphs date back to 1400 BC.

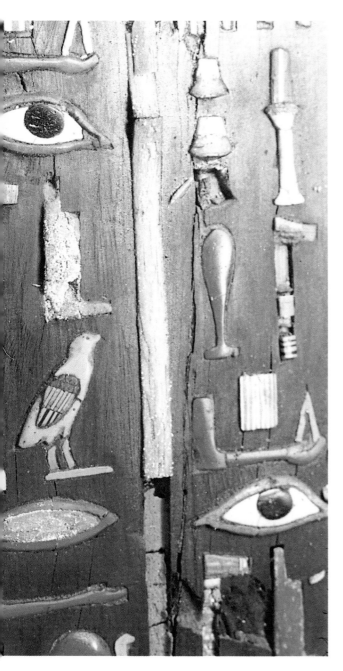

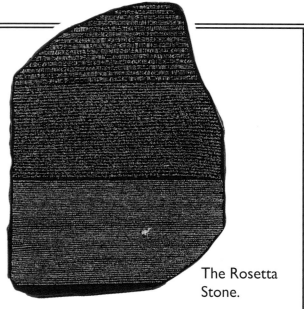

The Rosetta Stone.

For many years, nobody could read hieroglyphs. Then in 1799, in Egypt, a key discovery was made. A large stone slab – the Rosetta Stone – was found which bore an inscription in three different written languages Greek, hieroglyphs, and another Egyptian script called 'hieratic'.

A French scholar, Jean-François Champollion, used the Greek, which he could understand, to translate the meaning of hieroglyphs for the first time. However, because the ancient Egyptian language was not a true alphabet but was mainly written in ideograms, we will never know what it sounded like when spoken.

Left: These Egyptian hieroglyphs from the fourth century BC decorated the inside of an Egyptian wooden coffin.

This child is learning calligraphy at the Shanghai Palace of Culture in China. Writing Chinese characters is very difficult and takes many years to learn.

At the same time as the Egyptians invented hieroglyphs, the Chinese began to create their own writing system. Chinese writing developed using a combination of pictograms, ideograms and signs representing sounds. It has changed little over time and a young Chinese person today can read ancient as well as modern Chinese writing.

Each Chinese character stands for a whole word, so many thousands of characters are needed to write down the language. In all there are over 40,000 characters compared to the 26 letters in the Roman alphabet. Not all the characters are used in everyday life. A Chinese child will learn an average of 4,000 characters during the years he or she is at school. Some characters need as many as 32 strokes of the pen each. It is not surprising that writing Chinese is considered an art-form.

Western languages are written using an alphabet. An alphabet is different from pictograms or ideograms. Each letter of the alphabet stands for a particular sound. Letters which stand for sounds are known as phonetics. You can write down the letters C, A and T, and spell them out to make the word 'cat'.

The Phoenicians, who lived along the coast of Syria and Israel around 1800 BC, were the first people to have the idea of using letters to represent sounds. Using a mixture of symbols from earlier writing systems, they devised letters for the first true alphabet around 1050 BC.

The Phoenicians were great traders and sailors and their language spread with their travels around the world. Today's Greek, Arabic and Hebrew scripts, the Cyrillic alphabet used in Russia, and the Roman alphabet, which is used to write many of the world's languages including English, can all be traced back to the ancient script of the Phoenicians.

The Roman alphabet developed from the early Phoenician alphabet.

CODES AND SHORTHAND

There are ways to write down languages other than using alphabets, pictograms or ideograms. Examples include braille, shorthand, and secret codes.

Shorthand is a way of writing words and sentences very rapidly using *abbreviations*. The ancient Greeks developed a kind of shorthand but its use faded out during Roman times.

The shorthand used today was developed in Europe in the seventeenth century. The system was made simple and popular by Isaac Pitman in 1837 when he introduced his system of dots, dashes and curved lines. Many journalists and secretaries still use this system.

All writing systems have relied on visual signs to communicate language. However, a system to enable *visually impaired* people to read was invented in France in 1824 by Louis Braille. Braille, who had been blinded in an accident at the age of three, created an amazing system of small raised dots that stood for numbers, letters of the alphabet, and even music. The dots, punched into a page of thick paper, could be felt with the fingertips. Braille writing opened up a whole new world to visually impaired people.

This magazine cover shows shorthand being used. A skilled shorthand journalist can write down up to 120 words a minute.

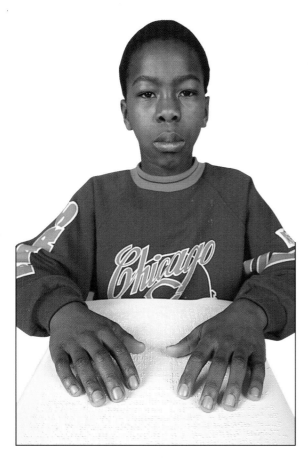

Above: This visually impaired boy is reading braille by touch, through his fingers.

The great advantage of writing is that it can be understood by other people, but sometimes this is a disadvantage if you want to keep information secret. Messages during wartime need to be kept secret from the enemy. Coded messages were widely used during the First World War to pass on sensitive information. Often the codes were disguised in letters or messages that would not appear suspicious to anyone else. Letters to relatives, grocery orders, and delivery notes often contained secret information passed on in code.

During the First World War, war-time messages were sent by code in order to keep information secret from the enemy.

HOW PAPER WAS INVENTED

Ancient Egyptians made the earliest form of paper from the papyrus reeds that grew along the banks of the River Nile. The oldest surviving papyrus was made more than 5,000 years ago.

Thin sheets were made from the stems of the papyrus plant, which were then wetted, pressed flat and dried in the sun. Scribes glued sheets of papyrus together into long lengths, then rolled them up into a scroll, ready to be written on.

The advantage of papyrus was that there was a plentiful supply of reeds available. Plantations were set up and run by the ancient Egyptian rulers. Papyrus was still expensive though so it was used for important documents such as religious scriptures and legal documents.

The holy book of the ancient Egyptians, the Book of the Dead, was written on papyrus around 1250 BC.

Trade with other nations spread the use of Egyptian papyrus to countries all around the Mediterranean. The demand for papyrus was huge. Egyptian supplies could not always be relied on outside Egypt. A suitable alternative was found in parchment which could be produced anywhere.

The ancient Chinese made paper by cutting bamboo (left), soaking it in water, and then pounding it to a pulp. After soaking with lime, the pulp was drained and dried and the new sheet of paper trimmed (right).

It is said that parchment was invented by King Eumenes when papyrus was in short supply between 197 and 158 BC. The word parchment comes from the name of his kingdom, Pergamum (now in modern-day Turkey). Parchment was made from animal skins, washed in water and lime, and then stretched on a frame. Although papyrus was still being used by the Romans in AD 273, parchment was the main writing material used in Europe until the fifteenth century.

The Chinese were the first to invent true paper. In AD 105, a Chinese man, Ts'ai Lun, soaked grass and leaves in lime water until they turned to pulp. Then he strained the mixture through a sieve and pressed it into flat sheets of paper. Later, the bark of mulberry trees (or bamboo) was used instead of the original soaked grass used by Ts'ai Lun. This made a very high quality white paper which became popular because it was cheaper to produce than silk.

For 700 years the Chinese kept the secret of paper-making to themselves. It was not until some paper makers were taken prisoner by Muslim invaders that the secret was passed on in return for their freedom. By 1400, there were paper-mills in Spain, France and Italy. In 1690, the first American paper-mill opened in Pennsylvania.

At first paper was very expensive. Paper became cheaper as more paper-mills opened, and pulped wood began to be used. Until the nineteenth century, paper was hand-made. One of the earliest paper-making machines was invented in 1798 in France.

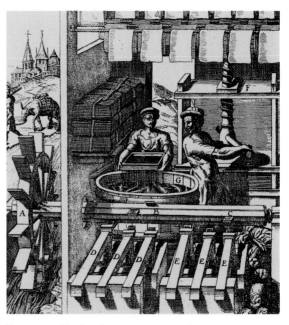

Paper-mills in the seventeenth century were powered by water-wheels.

Today, there are many types of paper, such as **boardbook** covers, tracing paper, **greaseproof** paper, newsprint and wrapping papers. Wood and other natural fibres such as cotton rags are ground up and mixed with water. This pulp is then heated in chemicals and washed and mixed with other substances which improve the quality of the paper. Presses squeeze most of the water from the wet pulp, and the newly-formed paper is then dried and wound into huge rolls. These are made by machines, which can be a kilometre or more in length.

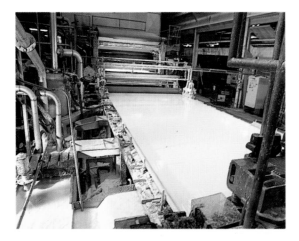

Part of a modern paper-making machine where the pulp is soaked in water.

EARLY WRITING TOOLS

Ancient civilizations had no pens or pencils as we know them today. People used materials they found around them, such as clay, bone, reeds, stone or tree bark, to hand-craft writing tools. Even sharks' teeth were used by the people of Easter Island in the Pacific.

The Sumerians wrote on **tablets** of wet clay with a **stylus** made from strong reeds, bone, or even metal. The way the end of the reeds were cut and sharpened determined the shape of the writing. Cuneiform writing was wedge-shaped without any curved strokes because of the shape of the reeds when cut.

Ancient Egyptians wrote hieroglyphs on temple walls with brushes made from thin strands of papyrus. Later, reed pens and brushes were used to write in ink on papyrus. Black ink was made from carbon and water for the first time. The reeds were split at the end to help the ink flow, in a similiar way to a modern pen nib.

The early writing tools in China called 'pi' were used to write in dark varnish or ink on bone, bamboo and silk. 'Pi' brushes were made of animal hair secured with silk thread to wooden handles.

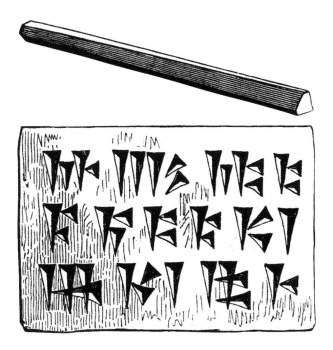

A drawing of a stylus and clay tablet.

A man and woman from Roman times holding a stylus, tablet and papyrus scroll.

Above: A Roman stylus and writing tablet. The wooden tablet was covered in wax which was then written on.

Ancient Romans wrote with iron or bronze styli on papyrus, parchment or on wooden tablets covered with wax. Wax-covered tablets were commonly used because the writing could be rubbed out and the wax could be written on again.

The first pencils were invented by the Romans. These were simply flat cakes of lead which were used to rule faint guidelines on stone ready for carving.

Around 1200, quill pens made from the strong flight feathers of a goose or other large bird began to be used in Europe. The hard tip of the feather was cut into a writing point and the natural hollow within the feather helped to hold the ink. Goose feathers were particularly suitable for quills because of the way they curve. The feathers on each wing curve in opposite directions. The feathers from a left wing are best suited to right-handed people and those from the right wing to left-handed people.

Pencils as we know them today were first introduced in France, in 1795. A wooden case was glued around a stick of *graphite* and clay. This helped to keep the writer's hand clean. The great advantage of pencil is that it can be rubbed out.

In the same way, children in the nineteenth century used chalk on slates to do their schoolwork because it could be rubbed out easily. However, writing in chalk or pencil is not as long lasting as writing made in ink.

This advert from 1927 encouraged people to buy Zeus pencils. Zeus pencils were made in Austria.

For around 600 years the quill pen remained the most popular writing tool in Europe. As late as the mid-nineteenth century, quill pens were still being used to write with in homes, schools and offices. But feathers tended to wear out quickly, and cutting new pens took time and skill. A stronger pen than the quill was needed.

PEN AND INK

In 1748, Johann Jantssen, an inventor from Aachen in Germany, created the first writing point made from steel. Others quickly followed, and inventors in France and Germany also claimed to have made the 'first' steel pen.

A modern pen nib being cut by a machine.

To begin with the new metal writing points, or nibs, were made by hand from thin strips of metal. The metal was hammered into a tube shape that fitted over the end of a wooden holder, then the writing tip was filed to a point. These proved to be very popular and by 1830, steel pen nibs were being produced by steam-powered machines in factories.

The invention of the steel pen nib brought about other changes. It was found that the ink that had been used with quill pens made the new metal pens go rusty. Inventors had to experiment with new inks. Some of them went bad quickly and smelled. Advances in chemistry and the invention of new dyes improved the quality of ink.

Steel pens were an improvement on quills but they had drawbacks. The writer had to keep dipping his or her pen into an ink-well.

HOW EARLY INKS WERE MADE

Ink has been used since ancient times, and was usually made of soot from oil lamps mixed with resin, gum, honey, borax, burnt almonds or even cows' urine. In ancient Egypt and China, black or red ink was often made in solid discs or sticks, rather like the solid paint in artists' palettes today. From Roman times until the nineteenth century, European ink was made from oak galls – growths on oak twigs made by insects – mixed with iron salts.

A Roman pen and ink-well made from bronze.

The first *fountain pen* had been made as far back as the tenth century, when the Arab leader, Caliph al-Mu'izz demanded a pen with its own supply of ink. His craftsmen made one for him from gold – but we are not told how well it worked. Fountain pens were rediscovered in the 1880s, but they were not very good. Ink did not flow out smoothly.

Modern pens.

George S. Parker, the founder of the Parker Pen Company.

Although there were earlier attempts, Laszlo Biro, a Hungarian, invented the first efficient ball-point pen in 1945. Even today the ball-point pen is widely known as a 'biro'. Ball-point pens differ from fountain pens in that they encase a tiny ball at the tip of the pen. As the writer moves the pen across the page the ball rolls and the ink, contained in a narrow plastic tube, is gently released on to the page. Often people have ideas at the same time but only one inventor is given the credit. Around the same time that Biro was working on his ideas, an American, Middleton Reynolds, developed and marketed a similar pen.

One of the first makers, George S. Parker (who was a lecturer), worked on improving the bad fountain pens supplied to his students. He started the Parker Pen Company, and by the end of the 1930s, he had become the world leader of the fountain pen industry.

An advert for ball-point pens dated 1888. Early ball-point pens did not write very well.

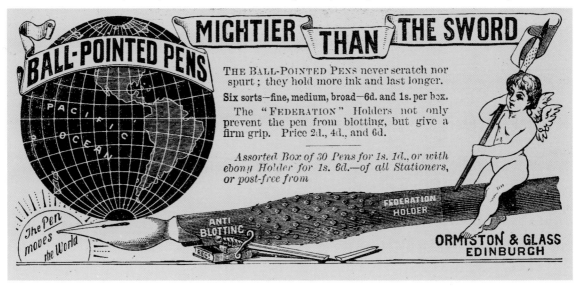

EARLY PRINTING

Before printing was invented books had to be written by hand. Scribes could take many months or even years to produce a single handwritten book. This made books very valuable. Many books were written and bound for the Christian Church by monks and nuns. Illuminated manuscripts from medieval times are among the most beautifully illustrated books in the world.

An illustration from a medieval manuscript. Here a monk risks a quick drink of ale.

The Chinese found out how to print using carved blocks of wood more than 1,000 years ago. Each wooden block had a whole page of characters on it.

Later, around AD 1045, the Chinese developed movable type made from pottery. This could be used to print characters in different arrangements over and over again.

The first Bible produced by Gutenburg contained over 1,200 pages.

By 1400, Europeans were printing with inked, wooden blocks just as the Chinese had done over 300 years earlier. A German goldsmith, Johannes Gutenberg, produced the first printing press in the town of Mainz in 1455.

Right: This eighteenth-century printing press is similiar to Gutenberg's original design.

The press was operated by hand and used metal type. Metal letters were arranged into words and sentences, then locked together within a frame. Ink was spread thinly over the surface, and paper was then pressed down on it to print a page of a book.

A *mechanical* printing press was invented in 1477. The idea spread rapidly and for the next 300 years printing presses changed little from Gutenberg's original design.

The first printers tried to imitate the handwritten style of the scribes and even had illuminated initial letters and handwritten decoration put on the pages. It took many years for printers to develop the modern typefaces of today.

JOHANNES GUTENBURG

Johannes Gutenberg was cheated by his partner, Johannes Fust. Fust became impatient with delays in starting up the press, and took legal action against Gutenberg only days before the first books were due to be published in 1457. Gutenberg was forced to give up his equipment and the first books printed on his press bore the name of Fust only. Other people made a fortune from Gutenberg's ideas, but the cheated inventor died in poverty.

An engraving of Johannes Gutenberg.

MAKING BOOKS

The Diamond Sutra – the earliest known book in the world – was printed in China in AD 868. Printed on it was a Buddhist prayer with intricate artwork designed around it.

The Buddha design was printed on a separate sheet of paper and then glued to the text in the form of a *scroll*. The scroll is over 5 metres in length. It is very different from the bound books of today.

The Diamond Sutra was printed using seven different printing blocks made of wood.

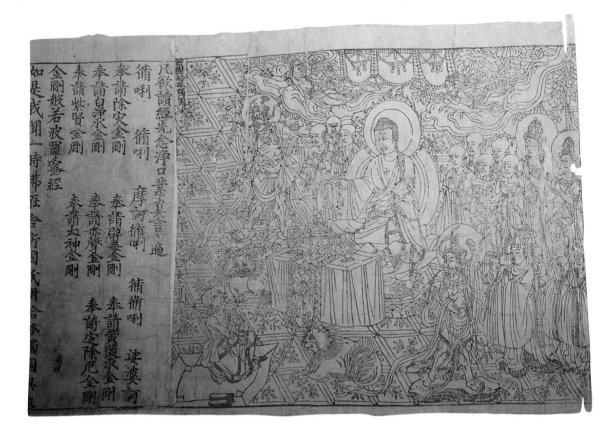

This codex comes from Mexico. The Aztecs (the ancient people of Central America) made it from beaten deer skin.

We owe the shape and form of books to the Romans. The Romans began to fold squares of parchment into sheets and sew them together on one side. This was better than scrolls because both sides could be written on. These early books called codices were widely used by AD 400.

William Caxton set up the first printing press in London in 1476. Caxton is famous for printing the first Bible in English, but he also printed novels, romances and educational books. Books were beginning to reach a much wider audience and cover a larger number of themes than ever before.

This Bible is known as the Lindisfarne Gospels. It was handwritten and bound in England in the year AD 698.

Binding of books is important to protect the pages from damage.

FROM GUTENBERG TO INFORMATION TECHNOLOGY

By 1811 a steam-powered printing press could produce 1,100 printed sheets an hour. However, the workers setting type by hand could only set 2,000 letters an hour, which held up the printing process.

American inventors developed faster ways of setting type by machine. Monotype machines set type letter by letter and linotype machines set a whole line of type in one operation. Linotype machines, introduced in 1886 in New York, could set over 6,000 letters an hour (three times as fast as by hand).

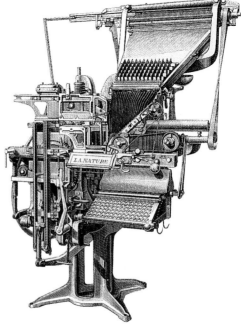

Above: A Linotype typesetting or 'composing' machine made in 1893.

This steam-powered, rotary printing press was invented in 1818.

It was not until 1867 that an American, C. Latham Sholes, invented the first typewriter. It was later marketed by the Remington Company, becoming popular in offices and homes throughout the world.

At first the typewriters were **manual**, which made them slow and heavy to use. By the 1950s and 1960s, electric typewriters had become common in offices. A fast typist could type more than 75 words a minute. Today, typing is done on computers or word processors.

A drawing of the first typewriter invented by C. Latham Sholes in 1867.

This Yost typewriter was made in 1912. It was a great improvement on earlier typewriters because its design was much smaller and easier to use.

The very first computer invented in the 1940s by IBM was so big that it had to be set up in a warehouse. It was not like the portable personal computers of today, some of which are small enough to fit inside a briefcase. Computers have now become vital to the smooth running of businesses and governments. A large **database** can store millions of pieces of written information which can be accessed by telephone from anywhere in the world.

INFORMATION TECHNOLOGY

Information technology has entirely revolutionized newspaper and book production. Each journalist or author writes directly onto a computer using a visual display unit. When the article or book is ready, a push of a button sends the information to the main computer where it is processed, ready to be printed.

Telephones and *optical fibres* can be used to pass information at the speed of light (around 300,000 km per second) around the world. Because of this *The Financial Times* and *Wall Street Journal* newspapers are able to print newspaper editions in a number of different countries at the same time.

This author is working at a visual display unit, more commonly known as a VDU.

TIMELINE

20000 BC Stone Age people begin to paint pictures on cave walls.	**3500 BC** The Sumerian people start to use pictograms as writing.	**3000 BC** Cuneiform writing evolves from pictograms in Mesopotamia.	**3000 BC** The ancient Egyptians develop hieroglyphs.	**3000 BC** The Chinese develop a writing system based on pictograms.

1000 BC The Chinese invent printing using carved wooden blocks.	**AD 105** In China paper is invented by Ts'ai Lun.	**AD 400** Early books or codices are widely used by the Romans instead of scrolls.		**AD 1045** The Chinese develop movable type.

1200 Paper-making begins in Europe. Quill pens are used for writing.		**1400** In Europe printing with carved wooden blocks replaces hand written manuscripts.	**1455** In Germany Johannes Gutenberg invents the first printing press using movable metal type.	**1476** William Caxton sets up the first printing press in England.

1477 The first mechanical printing press is invented.	**1748** The first steel pen is invented by Johann Jantssen in Germany.		**1811** The steam-powered printing press is invented.	**1824** Louis Braille invents the braille system of writing for the blind.

1867 An American, C. Latham Sholes, invents the first typewriter.	**1880s** The first efficient fountain pens are made.	**1886** Type is set by machine on Monotype and Linotype machines.	**1945** Computers are invented in the USA by IBM and the first efficient ball-point pen is invented.	**1980s** Typesetting machines are no longer needed as computers transform print production.

GLOSSARY

Abbreviation To make a word or sentence shorter.

Bamboo A plant with hollow woody stems which grows in hot countries.

Boardbook Thick paper similiar to cardboard used to cover books.

Codex (Codices) An early book with the pages stitched together down one side.

Database A computer storing large amounts of information.

Fountain Pen A type of pen with ink inside it which flows out so the writer does not have to dip the pen into an ink-well.

Graphite A type of carbon which is grey in colour and can be used to write with.

Greaseproof Paper Paper which does not let fat through it.

Information technology Speech, text and visual information fed into computers to be processed.

Manuscripts (Illuminated) Books or documents written and decorated by hand.

Mechanical Using machine power instead of doing something by hand.

Medieval The period of history between the fifth and fifteenth centuries AD.

Neanderthal Early humans who existed 35,000 years ago.

Optical fibres Fine glass fibres used to send messages.

Scribes People whose job it was to write.

Stylus (styli) A pointed writing tool made out of metal or reed plants.

Table A small, flat piece of wood or stone used to write on.

Technology Science that has practical value, especially in the business world, factories and workshops, and in art.

Typeface Design of letters and symbols used in printing.

Visually impaired A person with damaged or weakened eyesight.

BOOKS TO READ

Writing it Down, by Vicki Cobb, *Hodder & Stoughton* 1989

Aliki – Communication, by Aliki Brandenberg, *Methuen* 1993

Signs & Symbols – Writing and Numbers, by Jean Cooke, *Wayland* 1990

Club 99 – Write Away, by Viv Edwards, *A & C Black* 1991

The Story of Writing, by Brigitte Coppin, *Moonlight* 1992

PLACES TO VISIT

Victorian State Library
328 Swanston Street
Melbourne VIC 3000, Australia

The British Library
Great Russell Street
London WC1B 3DG, England

Stephen Leacock Museum
50 Museum Drive, Box 625
Orilla, Ontario L3V 6K5, Canada

INDEX

Numbers in **bold** indicate subjects shown in pictures as well as in the text.